Green Heart

Brinley Price

Q

First Published in Great Britain in 2023 by
Quacks Books
7 Grape Lane, Petergate, York, YO1 7HU
Tel: +44 (0)1904 635967
Email: design@quacks.info
Website: radiusonline.info
Quacks Books is an Imprint of Radius Publishing Ltd

A CIP catalogue record for this book is
available from the British Library.

ISBN Paperback: 978-1-912728-78-7

Set in ten point Baskerville with a page size of 148mm x 210mm
printed by offset lithography on one hundred gsm offset.

Foreword

Green Heart is both a hymn to, and a catalogue of, the natural diversity found in the small green spaces of our city. In these pages, the reader will find intrigue, contemplation and new insight into our natural world. Brinley Price's focus zooms from the minute detail of species to uplifting panoramas of urban nature and on into the effects these experiences can have on our wellbeing. Brinley knows the St Nicks local nature reserve as well as anyone we know; he has walked it and worked on it and now he honours it in this beautiful and enlightening series of poems. This is a book to treasure and come back to time after time.

Jo Young, St Nicks 2023

Contents

St Nicholas Fields

A brickyard first and then a landfill site;

Before that, by its name, perhaps a church;

Reminding me all passes, time is fleet

And to Death's brink the generations march.

Along this fertile hillock capped with clay

I make my way past primroses, birch leaves;

Though soon the life of speckled wood must fly

And surface green die back, what's deep survives.

This ground's foundations bear each winter blast;

Though kingfishers flash past and disappear,

The ancient beck flows through the clenching fist

Of ice each year, a trickle then a pour.

And I'll become this soil my soles now touch;

From me will thrust new sap, each Spring more rich.

New Beginning

I wish I'd listened to the soothing gulls

And felt the steady earth beneath my feet;

Instead I was confined by mind's grey walls

Down many years as though it was my fate.

And I regret the length I never heard

The subtle wisdom tuneful robins teach,

For simply sensing brings a rich reward

And living is to see, hear, smell or touch.

But I am human and was lured astray:

Through thinking's labyrinth I sought my foe

To strike him down, the self I would deny,

And I was lost and blind while cowslips blew.

And then, I grieve how late, the light shone in,

The blackthorn blossomed white and life began.

St. Aidan's

I've never seen a flock of coots before:

As black as coal from this once open cast

They dash across the track to reedy shore

Beaten by waves because of biting blast.

This grassland's flooded now, become a lake

On which we spot dark shapes of golden eye

Despite the wind-flung sleet that makes us ache.

A cormorant wings away below wide sky;

Proud on a rock it perched till we trudged near,

Now flaps above the water wild and bleak.

A pair of greylag geese swim off in fear

As though we came to cull not life to seek.

But it's the cold from which I fly, inside;

You stay to watch a kestrel swoop, storm-ride.

Natural Grace

Once conscientious but not conscious, fully,

I sold my soul to goodness knows what lord

And found him out to be a rule-bound bully

Though to begin with my sad spirit soared.

Work gave me pride and purpose at the start

But then rose rage, anxiety and guilt

And so I came to see our ways must part

As flowers of peace and joy began to wilt.

Now some say I am selfish, lazy too,

Since now I gaze where maple leaves are gold,

Or silver with the frost, less often do

Good works than they whose sorry lives are sold.

"The world would end were all like you, so base,"

Censure these saints— who pay a greater cost,

Dead in their hearts since blind to signs of grace,

To veins on this pale leaf now traced by frost.

Convolvulus

Untwining bindweed from the twigs of trees

Is like a meditation in a maze;

At first the mind revolts as more it sees

Then it finds quiet and its spirits raise.

By letting go and letting be it grows

Absorbed in this quaint puzzle that it solves;

The hand moves quicker and its movement flows;

There's satisfaction as the mess resolves.

These tendrils, as they climb this ash, grow fine;

Some, dying as they rise, are limbs snapped off;

Some weave together and their strengths combine

And to this knotwork my naff hat I doff.

These curious spirals lure me in and far

From fearful convolutions of the mind,

From thoughts more twisting, tangling, than weeds are,

And clarity returns as stems unwind.

Vegetation

As I grow old I start to vegetate,

Become a garden thick with vegetation;

I've gone to seed now, having flowered of late;

Just being is my present occupation.

And yesterday I potted cowslip seeds;

The sun was blazing and my mind was calm;

A simple humble task is all one needs,

To just sit still and hold life in one's palm.

So many years I built the world's machine—

I've gained a Perspex trophy for my toil—

But now I roam through spaces that are green

And plant these tiny living things in soil.

And peace and joy are now once more the soul's;

The hidden meaning of it all I see,

That was obscured by clouds of rules and goals:

The purpose of existence is to be.

Pruning Saplings

A pole, a pair of secateurs, a cord;

The branches bend but we can't hear them cut;

Now Steve falls off the fence and we applaud,

And yet we hope he hasn't hurt his nut.

Our cutters cannot reach the highest twigs,

A bramble forest standing in our way,

And Stuart's given up and smokes his cigs,

And only Freya bravely joins the fray.

A bramble thorn has pierced my gardening glove,

My finger throbs yet I come back each week;

Is it the ecotherapy I love—

Or is it throbbing fingers that I seek?

And yet Steve's backward roll was much admired;

And by the pruning gadget, little use,

Our curiosity was so inspired,

Some mad inventor obviously let loose.

These saplings will grow lusher now they're lopped;

They pose, a row of grateful amputees;

The bramble army's fast advance is stopped

And we have stopped for biscuits, coffees, teas.

And we'll be back next week since we are keen,

Despite the piercing thorns and backward rolls,

To make this corner of York City green—

With useless tools like secateurs on poles...

April Fool

When I strode out the light was fierce,

The sky deep blue; my heart took wing

Where in a wood a robin sang;

I paused to feel its primal force.

But further on the sun's face hid

And I was lashed by snow and hail;

Corroded gold the daffodil;

A sorry cowslip drooped its head.

As though to cheer themselves a flock

Of sparrows chirped, a frantic rave,

But could not please me as I strove

Past blackthorns blossoming white smoke.

How like the weather of the mind

That these past weeks of spring has turned

From calm to storm, though unforwarned

And unbeheld its cause or end.

Yet now more bright and more serene

I see the path ahead, endure

The brutal blasts that are in store,

Enjoy the transient waves of sun.

For Nature's motions may inspire

To bear the bane that's thought and felt;

Where dandelion petals wilt

New ones like yellow rays appear.

The Woodlouse

The woodlouse creeps with purpose that's unknown

Across this weathered table where I cut

These twigs of yew and plant them in a pot;

I too work slowly this chill afternoon.

It's armoured body does not gleam; dull grey

This tiny tank, this fairy knight's stout horse

Whose many legs, they struck by warlock's curse,

Get nowhere fast – as often so do I.

Where does it travel to on paths that wind?

Does it patrol this plain to find its food?

I also have a goal and yet am glad

To still my mind, be simply eye and hand.

We'll see these cuttings grow without a thought,

Their aim the sun, their starting place the soil;

No individual and divided will

Deflects their movement nor blots out their light.

And woodlouse, yew twigs, I, we better thrive—

I single-minded, they uncursed with mind

And single— each to past and future blind,

Each pure in being, nakedly alive.

Potting Cowslips

The compost golden brown in April light;

The sprouting cowslips, clumps of tiny ears

Attuned to birdsong, goldfinch and great tit.

Above my head clear blue, a gull that soars,

But I'm below, my fingers in the soil

And struggling to replant these roots like wires.

And yet I know that, given time, I will

And pause to hear the great tit's seesaw song,

Finding that earth's a doorway to the soul.

They'll grow, these little lives that tightly cling

To dark and damp, they'll yield their yellow flowers.

I sit below this willow's overhang—

These budding twigs— and all around me choirs;

I toil but breathe, and life is in my hands,

Spring in my heart despite my growing years.

After the Easter's bitter rains and winds,

This moisture-fed and sun-empowered growth.

Cherish this day of cowslips' gleaming fronds

And vibrant strands that mark the year's late birth.

Remembering St. Nicholas's Fields

Written during lockdown

Now sadness fills my core

Although this afternoon

Is brilliant blue and gold.

Like water still and chill

Pain drowns me from inside

Despite the loving light

As summer gilds the panes

Of windows, presses through

To hold me, soak me deep.

I haven't left my home

All week, my walks postponed—

Life beckons me outdoors

To where red campion

And bird's-foot-trefoil flower

Carnelions, amethysts,

And where tall grasses foam

And flow and hiss, like sea

That ebbs from shingle shore.

For mind contains all worlds

And only to recall

Some sights and sounds is joy.

Noli Me Tangere,

Newly emerged, a Burnet moth,

You struggled from your dull cocoon

On a tall stalk of grass.

Now resting on a human hand

You seem to feel serene and safe

Or merely warm we guess.

The sun is strengthening your wings

Of glossy grey with six red spots

Flickering as they dry.

Poised on the very edge of flight

Are you reluctant to desert

Warmth of humanity?

And do you sense solicitude

That seeps from nature-lover's skin

Or eyes that gaze with care?

Or is it fear of snapping beak

Swooping down from the lethal sky

That keeps you clinging here?

Rather, the lassitude of one

Still climbing out of pupal sleep,

Finally stirring, gone;

A sort of metamorphosis

Cocooned by fingers, thumb and palm,

A miracle of sun.

In the John Lally Community Wood

Throughout my miserable life

I have tried to do what was right

Though frequently I have erred.

But now I am sixty two

With less to anticipate

I enjoy this winter blaze:

For light is bursting through

The now most fortunate gaps

In this dark denuded wood.

Decimated indeed

By a desecrating storm

It is my sanctuary still;

It is my present church

With its piers, arches and vaults,

Austere, Cistercian now

And yet in summer ornate

And painted glowing green,

In autumn golden and red.

In spring I heard a choir,

A canon of birds and now

A robin's solo hymn.

To a wretched one comes love,

His God, Salvation on Earth:

The Grace of sights and sounds.

Haiku

A bright bumble bee,

Catching the sun in its hairs,

Holds onto summer.

How sweet in autumn

The robin's song among songs—

Soon the only song.

Bearing Fruit

Fruit trees need nursing,

The clicking of metal blades

Correcting misgrowth.

We stand on compost,

Its heaps unstable platforms,

And wield our loppers.

New to pruning trees,

Over-enthusiastic,

We reach for the sky.

The topmost branches

Are safe from our stretching arms—

Our loppers snap air.

Nearer to the ground

The broken or malformed limbs

Are amputated.

A soft snapping sound

Then twigs plunge through the cold air

To merge with the soil.

Later, while we sit,

Our labour's elation past,

Our legs grow heavy.

Car's distant thunder—

Then a robin's bright singing

Evaporates gloom.

At Castle Howard

Blazing with rage

I blunder through the arboretum

Then, seeing the trees aflame with autumn,

Become as calm as this lake

Where mallards contentedly chuckle.

A fly agaric, youth's orange-red,

Carries me back to laughter, adventure

Darkening into nightmare—

But then the nuthatch's 'wheat, wheat, wheat'

Awakes me into the now.

Rain drops are pattering through oak leaves;

Below, a yellow-green frog is hopping away

As the present escapes me and thoughts beat down on my head,

Memories heavy as lead,

And yet it is not too late: still dandelions shine.

A Caucasian wing nut has painterly bark:

Nature has used a palette knife on its canvas.

Innumerable long-tailed tits are flitting through branches.

In boggy ground are green umbrellas.

From car park gravel grow shaggy ink caps for pens.

The plop of sweet chestnuts landing in leaf-litter,

A peacock feather like patterned glass,

A breeze that fondles my cheek, the fragrance of grass,

Are like a boat that bears me from stormy waters

Back to the harbour of life and love.

Donna Nook

The eerie song of seals:

The soulful demands of pups,

A mother's ghostly warning,

A bull's belligerent bellow.

A massive male with bloody neck,

Its laboured breathing, so near,

And, far away, shapes like shadows

Struggle towards a grey thread of sea.

Across the expanse of grass and mud

They are scattered like bulky sandbags

Or giant slugs, their tan and white and black,

Their drab motley.

The cold is keen and yet they sunbathe

Below a pale blue November sky

Where gulls incessantly circle

And crows are flapping about.

An occasional battle of snarling bulls

But otherwise daylight slumber,

Their bodies bloated with fish,

Their black eyes many fathoms deep.

'Ne'er Shed a Clout'

Painfully cold

After yesterday's deluge

We search for rare snake's-head fritillary

But find it washed away.

No orange-tips today

Although last week there was a host of them;

Instead a dull crowd of wood-pigeons,

A drab unsinging dunnock.

Yet cowslips shyly show their gold,

Bluebells hug to themselves their clustered sapphires

And native primroses shine up at us

Like earth-bound suns.

And tansy ventures inches above ground

Although we cannot see as yet

Those wings of iridescent metal,

Its banqueting beetle.

So while our bodies smart

As the wind whips us through our clothes

Our souls are well, hearts high,

Before the green rowan banishing ill.

We pause awhile despite the brutal chill,

Behold the hawthorn leaf's miniature tree,

The still-clenched May flower's

Tiny white fist, a new-born child's.

Green Heart

Green-hearted I walk out a little way

From where I live amidst these loud dull streets

To where is peace and joy, of where we say,

Beset by a dead world, York's green heart beats.

And where we sense quick sap, like human blood

In human veins, thrust up from clayey soil,

Up through lithe hazel tree to pregnant bud,

We are reborn from killjoy care and toil.

Where teasels store in leaves half swords, half cups,

Rainwater, though high summer's heat bears down,

And motley goldfinch on rough seedhead sups,

We find our faces cleared of worry's frown:

From there a smile beams down on cranesbill's blue;

York's green heart beats, our green hearts beating too.

Tree Creeper

i

Brown-coated you slide up a rough tree trunk,

Ascending to indomitable height,

Stare down on human brutes so basely sunk

While your pale breast's illumined by Spring light.

In a wild spiral up and up you climb,

A little bird but one with big ambition:

To get to heaven yet in spite of time

And gravity's iron laws, your fervent mission.

You make me think of us chained down to Earth

And yet who seek transcendence of our dust,

Whether through resurrection or rebirth,

Who strive to climb by faith or being just—

But are like you, proud bird, who soon must fall

Because of Nature ruling over all.

ii

I saw you in the Spring, the light intense,

A morning when a wave of heat surged in,

When waking wildlife pleasured every sense

And made we humans feel we were its kin.

You rose like green stems bursting into flower,

Climbed up a tree and mimed its upward thrust;

And yet I knew that death's despotic power

Would halt your climb, your form return to dust.

Yet climbing, and not having reached the top,

Is your salvation, heaven, little bird

Brown-coated and pale-breasted, so don't stop—

Although you won't, your work by instinct stirred.

It's in the action not its end we rise,

Defeat Earth's tyranny and reach the skies.

Comma

An angel made of dust, a butterfly,

A fluttering redness mirroring my heart,

Adorned my breast as though a painter's art

Had daubed it there and, while I did not try,

I found a treasure, rather one found me:

Its precious metal bore the rust of time,

Soon to be stolen, such is Nature's crime,

As are all joys that come to us for free.

And as I watched it fly, a glowing ember

Of blazing Earth and then a russet leaf

Torn from a tree branch early in November,

I felt a fierce delight for life so brief

But beautiful and worthy to remember

Though lost, its afterglow beyond all grief.

Observance

We saw a sparrow hawk, its flap and glide,

Its circling and its disappearing trick,

And certainly that was a stroke of luck

But not for any bird on which it preyed.

We saw a great tit in the hazel twigs

And heard its song: two oscillating notes

Metallic-sounding like a saw that cuts

Through air, a clown that humorously nags.

We heard the fearful clicking of a wren,

Saw goldfinch pecking teasels for seeds' prize

And blackthorn flowers shelter last year's sloes,

Before our sharp-eared watchful walk was done.

We saw and heard, we did not think a lot

Nor brood at all; our heads with life were filled,

Our senses wakened and our worry foiled,

Our mental darkness washed away by light.

Marsh Marigolds

Marsh marigolds translucent to the light,

Their petals fine, as yellow as the sun;

They quiver, envying the Brimstone's flight

Because the mud in which they root they shun.

The pond smells stagnant yet, imprisoned there

Within its slum, it seems that some grow rich:

Like these street urchins with blond heads, who stare

At sky for whose abundant blue they itch.

In my Spring also I was kept below

Among the pond life, struggling to survive

Yet striving to escape, at least to grow,

Aspiring in my way to shine and thrive.

But now I watch the bee these flowers feed,

Its dark head dipping in their cups of gold,

And see not will to power but mutual need,

My mind made humbler as I grow more old.

Dandelion

A dandelion: beauty but not rare,

A flower composed of countless little flowers

Like rays of sunlight or like yellow hair,

A vision every spring that never sours;

And when I gaze at one it gazes back

And, as it makes me smile, it smiles on me;

And, teaching me 'to have' is still 'to lack',

It is a lesson on the verb 'to be';

And like the Universe itself: each small

And humble part an image of the whole;

In every fragile thing the mighty all,

Nature in flesh and blood and God in soul.

Yet by late summer flower has gone to seed,

Its head a puff of smoke to disappear,

As though by dying back the life is freed

To multiply by April days next year.

After the Storm

After this winter gale has loosed its power

So many trees lie fallen in its wake—

And yet we see the snowdrop's little flower

In the retreating tempest fiercely shake,

And this gives hope that trees that still may tower

Will soon be green and gone the cold's dull ache.

The alder's cones lie scattered in the mud;

Two tree trunks smashed through some poor neighbour's fence,

By blasts brought low; the beck is in full flood

Like feelings of our loss now so immense.

Yet we discover bold and sticky bud

Of lone horse chestnut and our gain we sense.

There from behind a branch a nuthatch peeks

And, playing peek-a-boo, retires from view;

A dray high up a jumpy squirrel seeks

As if escaping from our nosy crew

With our intrusive stares as each one speaks

Excitedly of seeing something new.

Then we return indoors, sit round warm stove,

Drink tea, eat cake and talk of future days

When under leafy canopy we'll rove

And learn a little more of Nature's ways;

Further from when against life's winds we strove,

Now mending, once again our heads we raise.

Blackcaps

Most folk have secret dreams of glory:

Being ones who've failed, been blamed,

We lift ourselves upon fantastic wings

And to the world each sings.

But listening to a flock of birds,

A choir of blackcaps in the trees,

Their hymn to life, their frenzy of elation,

Stirs some to contemplation:

Each striving for itself all stay

A musical community,

Like we who are small sights in one great seeing,

A universal being;

And flitting tensely, twig to twig,

Their little wings disturbed by urges,

Joined these fowl perform a village dance

Though to the tune of chance.

We choral group, we dancing troupe,

While each one also stands alone,

Losing again let's take the larger view

Though only partly true,

Because such descant sounds more bright,

Less petty than our songs of self,

And those who hear it on this earth of war

May seek the skies and soar.

The Path

A narrow path, a stab of fear

Now someone else is walking near;

We fail to see the other soul

Is one for whom the bell might toll

And one like us, a human peer.

To self alone our worry points,

A sad old self with aching joints

And when it's gloomy like today

Our bestial nature we obey—

Our spiritual when sun anoints!

Red campion and tufted vetch

Entice us from the self, that wretch;

Shrill power of the tiny wren

Draws us away a moment when

Inside the head's a frightening sketch;

And lured by light, by tinkling beck

Borne far away from nation's wreck,

We smile at others, faces bright

Or shaded by deep green, brief height

Where horror shrieks below, mere speck.

Thus Nature heals the mind's disease

And the observing spirit frees

And where the wild geraniums blaze,

Touched by midsummer sun, we gaze

At meadow grasses' waves and these.

Litter-Picking

To pick up rubbish means that we're not trash—

Although we're daft not doing it for cash!

Corroded saucepans, plastic, broken glass,

These are the litter-picker's badge of class—

Perhaps rich debutantes should have a bash!

Gin bottles, mattress springs, smashed plates come free;

The more we pull them up the more we see;

Disposing safely of a peril— 'sharps'—

One person gives his verdict when he 'parps'—

To a politician's speech on drugs the key!

One picker thinks he's found a bronze-age hoard—

Or says he has because he's feeling bored;

But this reminds us that a rubbish pile

Will bring to archaeologists a smile

Far in the future, though today we snored.

While Nature gazes on with face serene—

Blithe snowdrops, blackthorn blossom, hawthorn's green—

We grow more frantic now we're near our break,

Because of messy humankind backs ache.

We find a thing unspeakable, obscene...

Coffee and cake revive the sickening soul

As we regret we played such noble role:

Fitting for serfs it now appears to us;

Posh ladies sniff us on the homeward bus—

Such civic virtue takes a heavy toll!

Bolton Abbey

As raindrops pattered on the leaves, our clothes,

We walked along a wooded slope and saw

Spring's bluebells, stitchwort, also cuckoo flowers,

Heard willow warblers in the trees around

And smelled wild garlic massed beside a beck

That spilled across a road. Close by the ford

A dipper with pale breast, dark back, God thank,

Was feeding in a hollow of the bank.

A sandpiper was glimpsed where River Wharfe

Was shallow, rocky and meandering

Through fields of sheep above which ruins loomed.

And on the foaming waters were beheld

A goosander, grey wagtail, mandarin duck

More visible past noon, the sun intense,

The rainclouds and the showers paused awhile

As joy expanded down this country mile.

Then, settling on Carl's coat, a nomad bee

That glistened in this morning interlude

And then was gone, reminded me how brief

Epiphanies that pierce the sense-world are.

Yet, like the light that broke through roof of rock

And warmth embracing us still damp from rain,

They turn the mundane water into wine.

We know and are, for moments, the divine.

Afternoon and Evening

A robin's electric treble;

Long-tailed tits

Darting this way and that,

Their little wings vibrating;

Playful squirrels

Jumping from branch to branch;

The tiger stripes of light and shade:

This joy and peace I sacrificed

To an idol of perfection

Angering the mind

Against the body,

Against itself.

I sold my soul, my birthright,

And gained pain.

A bonfire rages,

Flames gnaw through wood,

A snapping noise,

Swirling pulses of smoke:

Thus I consumed myself,

Striving to rise

To a sky unreachable.

Patience is better

And humility

And simple faith,

Here by a many-voiced rapid,

Hearing the duck's contented quacking,

Watching a low and amber sun

Through trees with few leaves left.

My Sixtieth Autumn

Now I am getting old

And now my body is like a child

Demanding everything—

I'll go outside where it's cold

And hear once more the bullfinch call,

Its creaking gate, and see again

The patchwork leaves,

This autumn now my own.

I'll drink the chill rain through my skin

Because my heart needs nourishment,

Because my judging head

Numbers our every sin

And can't repent nor yet grow wise.

I'll sense the rosehip's red,

The shrivelled haw, the mouldy sloe

That hold the seeds of Earth's new year.

I'll hope I too will rise once more,

With spring will be reborn

Still ageing, frail

But willing to live on

Because the blackthorn wears her white.

Yet now I'll merge with murk

Like gulls that glide through gloomy skies

And I not liking this

But being here at home,

Treading through wet and fecund mud.

Trees

The storm inside my mind roared on for days;

I tried to ride its waves that seemed immense,

Watch gloomy clouds race past,

Feel lightning hurt rip through me but embrace it.

And then I met the elder,

Its tortured trunk, its evil-smelling leaves,

Yet utterly alive,

Giving life to delicate jelly ear.

I gazed on weird goat willow

Winters had worn down,

Its lower branches dead, some broken off,

But high above the thinnest spray of green.

And then an ash the world had darkened,

Lichens embroidering its aged body;

A sycamore's huge hands that tar spots ate

And yet that caught the pouring light.

I heard the poplar's pain

As the wind wrenched its limbs

But saw it rise above its torment,

Reaching high because its roots drove deep.

And lastly the laburnum,

Its poisonous yet beautiful cascade,

Its blooms malignant but like amethysts,

Leaving no room for rage.

In Mid March

We saw the bumble bees

Among the primroses'

Vividly painted faces

Beside the woodland path,

Thin hawthorns' scanty green

The backdrop to their dance.

For like an acting troupe

With many varied parts,

The buff-tail, carder, tree

Performed their ancient drama,

Ritual of pollination

Far from fires of summer.

We heard the gentle drone

Of this strange musical

Humbler than prima donna

Blackbird high in a tree

That, grudged enough applause,

Fell silent, flew away;

These players more subdued,

Their's yet more serious art

Fitting to this chill month,

This very verge of Spring:

Their costumes tawny, black,

Their murmuring, not song.

Jelly Ears

The elder is all ears,

Is wise enough to listen

To December's rant,

The loud and harsh debate

Of magpies' parliament.

A brown translucency

Ears dangle from a branch,

The elder bearing fruit

That's rotten or exotic.

I've heard they're good to eat

And kind of cute perhaps

Like children's ears, attentive

To a teacher's yell;

It's weird that elder has

Such ears in old age still.

Or are they jellyfish

In winter's chilly deep,

Torn by the latest storm

And, used to warmer seas,

Harbouring here from harm?

They tremble slightly but

To the bough's wizened bark

Their being's glue holds fast.

Whose birthday treat is this

Tremulous jelly feast?

Outside

Wake up and smell the wild flowers:

Chicory, corn marigold, tufted vetch;

One can be freed from fear,

Forget self-doubt and shame

And shed one's rage, if only for a while.

Seeking the sweetness

Of buddleia's purple blooms

A flock of peacock butterflies

Entices one away

From a quarrel inside one's head.

A blast of sunlight

Turns the pond water luminous,

The sedge's green intense

And chases the shadows away from the mind

That now may gaze outwards.

No longer locked into itself,

Chained to an endless treadmill,

One's spirit leaps the gulf to where

The broad-bodied chaser is darting about,

A wind-blown willow is beckoning.

A pigeon's grey explosion,

Less frightening than one's own brain power,

Snatches one out of one's shouting whirlpool,

One's bellowing labyrinth,

Opens into the spacious grace of now.

Restoration

Wretched weather today,

The sky a window pane grimed over,

A short ration of light.

But yesterday, a brilliance revealed

Bee orchid, vetch and yellow loosestrife,

A meadow crowded with beauties.

Between their heads the ringlet butterfly

Threaded dull but quick

As though it wove that wildflower tapestry.

At Askham Bog the ragged robin

Mirrored my torn but vivid soul

Borne away by an emperor dragonfly.

A royal fern taught me

The history of living things

More deeply rooted than human myths.

But over the car park a kestrel

Brought home what still hung over me:

The illness then briefly healed.

And now beneath a swamp of clouds

I bring to the mind's stagnating surface

These gleaming treasures, these images of health.

Blue Tit

A blue tit pecking the bark of a birch,

Probably rooting out insects,

Is climbing up the trunk's intense white.

We watched it while we sat outdoors

In brilliant early summer

As though our vision was suddenly focused.

Awake to an avian symphony

Immediately we fell silent

And were for a moment all eyes and ears

And held our breaths while the breeze sighed out

As though the world breathed for us,

The canopy shaken, a tambourine.

And now that I sit alone, uneasy,

Far from that peace and joy,

Surrounded by the gloom of my thoughts,

I bring it all to mind once more:

The light that lifted our hearts,

The breath that inspired us, songs that soothed;

And what gave us wonder: the silk-skinned tree,

Its countless tiny green cymbals

And, almost as small, the bird mountaineer.

Sanctum

I'm in my home alone and feeling sad,

Although this radiant day should bring me joy;

I grieve for small success that I once had,

For thwarted dreams I've cherished since a boy.

Then I recall the music on our walk:

The orchestra of birdlife all around,

A blackbird's solo cutting short our talk,

Rising above the rest, a blessed sound.

We saw the meadow cranesbill blue as sky,

The soil-enriching clover, red and white,

Over the pond the azure damselfly

And common hawker gleam in golden light.

And far away from labour, striving, care,

We briefly held that pearl beyond compare.

The Pond

The raindrops splashing, rippling this brown pond,

The island made of bright marsh marigolds

And wispy mace, are sights of which I'm fond;

My joy is in quick nymphs still water holds.

My loves are newts who can't return my love

With their cold blood, their lives among the lank

Dull strands where they may spurn the world above;

My eyes meet ox-eye daisies on far bank.

Though I'm a creature of the land, the light,

I've depths of darting shadow, tangling weed;

While I admire broad-bodied chaser's flight,

Imagination dives where larvae feed.

When dipping in the pond or in my mind,

Tadpoles not monsters of the deep I find.

Tansy Beetles

In memory of Anneliese Emmans Dean

On tansy leaves medicinal in scent

Those little beads of iridescent metal

Like jewellery on which much work was spent

By Nature, more it seems than on mere petal.

Can humble leaf or common bird compete?

Not even starling with exultant shimmer

Can vie with these live gems we rarely meet,

That keep their sheen though April skies grow dimmer.

And as beside the River Ouse we stroll,

Along the tow path here at Clifton Ings,

Since spotting two we find we're on a roll

Now more appear: redundant gleaming wings.

Yet since this treasure soon must rust away

We, worldly wise, enjoy it while we may.

Acknowledgements

I would like to express my profound gratitude:

To David Hammond who set to music two Haiku included in this collection.

To Marianna Michell who printed my sonnet 'Comma' in the magazine *Unlock* edited during the Covid pandemic.

To Kathy Sturgess, previously Ecotherapy manager at St Nicks, who first took on the project of helping me put together this book.

To Eleanor Tookey, Ecotherapy mentor at St Nicks, who word-processed these poems and corrected the typos.

To Jo Young, nature-based wellbeing manager at St Nicks, who advised me on the practicalities of bringing a book into print and supervised the process.

To all the staff, volunteers and participants at St Nicks, without whom this book and the good experiences expressed in it would not be possible.

To my sister, Dr Carolyn Price, who listened to many of these poems and gave me her sage advice.

To Dave Mair, Tracie Bailey and Laurie Farnell who instilled in me the courage to put my poems in print.